Soft Toys

Soft Toys

Delphine Davidson

B. T. Batsford Limited   London

Charles T. Branford   Company
Newton   Massachusetts

To Ann and Elaine

First published 1971
7134 2651 9

Library of Congress Catalogue Card Number
Branford ISBN 8231-5028-3

Filmset by Keyspools Ltd, Golborne, Lancashire
Printed and bound in Great Britain by
C. Tinling & Co. Limited London and Prescot

for the publishers
B. T. Batsford Limited
4 Fitzhardinge Street   London W1   and
Charles T. Branford Company
28 Union Street   Newton Centre   Massachusetts 02159

CONTENTS

INTRODUCTION

There is a wide selection to choose from in this book, from soft toys to a hobby-horse with pole, reins and bells and three larger toys for children to sit upon, climb over or stand on! The last mentioned toys are rather more difficult and more strenuous to make but are well worth the effort as children adore them. The toys are arranged in order of difficulty, so a beginner is advised to start with one of the toys at the beginning of the book before attempting the more difficult ones.

GENERAL INSTRUCTIONS

Making the pattern

Large sheets of white, brown or graph paper are required for making the patterns. If plain white or brown paper is used, draw lines with a ruler and a set square or a piece of card with a right angle, first vertically the correct distance apart and then horizontally to form squares. The size of the squares depends on the pattern chosen and is clearly marked on each diagram. If graph paper is used rule lines both horizontally and vertically to form squares to the correct size, using the lines on the graph paper as a guide. Copy the patterns from the diagram very carefully, working from square to square so that the pieces fit together properly. If larger or smaller toys are required, either increase or decrease the size of the square accordingly. It is advisable, however, to keep to the size stated for the hobby-horse and the three children's pouffes as these are the correct size for playing with and sitting upon.

Mark all the details — the name of the pattern and toy — on to each piece. The arrow indicates the direction of the material. The small black triangles mark the points for snipping the seam.

All the patterns in this book have turnings allowed. The smaller soft toys have 6 mm ($\frac{1}{4}$ in.) allowed, and the children's pouffes have an allowance of 13 mm ($\frac{1}{2}$ in.), unless otherwise stated in the individual instructions.

If the patterns are to be used more than once, it is advisable either to draw the patterns directly on to thin white cardboard or to glue the paper patterns to some cardboard and then cut carefully round each shape. Cardboard patterns are much more durable than paper ones and are easier to mark round with pencil or tailor's chalk on to the materials to be cut out.

Store the patterns in large envelopes, with the name of the toy and the number of pattern pieces on the outside.

This ensures that none of the smaller patterns are missing before starting to cut.

Fabrics

Most of the toys given here can be made from purchased remnants of material or left over pieces from dressmaking or curtain making. A search through the bit-bag will probably reveal some suitable materials. An old piece of good material will make a far more lasting toy than a cheap material bought especially for the purpose. The best parts of discarded articles of clothing are often ideal for toys. If material has to be purchased, it follows that the more attractive it is, the more attractive the toy will be when completed.

Here are some suggestions of suitable materials for some of the toys. The three children's pouffes require a very firmly woven, strong material that does not fray easily, if they are to withstand hard wear and tear. It may be possible to use the best parts of old curtains or part of a bedspread for these, as long as the materials have been washed and show no sign of rotting fibres. If a material with a large repeating pattern is chosen for the pouffes or for any of the other toys, match the pattern where possible for a professional result. This will probably mean that more material is required than stated in the individual toy instructions.

The otter and the penguin are very attractive in fur fabrics, but as these are very expensive to buy, other materials may be used with equal success. Velvet or tweed is suitable for the body pieces and either white velvet or the best part of an old white blanket for the front body gussets. If fur fabric is chosen for these two toys, it is preferable to choose a washable type of fur fabric, such as nylon or courtelle. To make the toys completely washable, stuff them with foam chips and sew on the felt details. They can then be washed and spin-dried in a washing machine.

There are various types of fur fabrics. Some are constructed with a woven technique and some with a knitted structure. The woven fur fabric is often known as baize and is fairly easy to work with but does not wash well. The knitted fur fabric which is generally made of nylon or courtelle washes very well, but it is not as easy to cut out and sew together as it tends to stretch considerably. If this type of fur fabric is used, it is essential to tack all the pieces together before sewing. If the toys are to be machine stitched, it is helpful to place some tissue paper underneath the fabric to minimize the problem of the bottom piece stretching more than the top piece.

The fish, giraffe, hobby-horse and dachshund have a fairly simple basic shape. They require a very attractive material, preferably suggestive of the animals natural markings. Choose a printed fabric rather than a plain one for these toys. Towelling, viyella or remnants of cotton prints or furnishing materials are all suitable. The dachshund is very successful if a multi-coloured striped fabric is used, with the stripes running round the body. It is essential to match the stripes carefully along all the seams for a professional result. Because of this, more material than stated in the instructions may be required.

Some of the man-made fabrics such as tricel, nylon and crimplene are unsuitable for toymaking. Shiny materials such as silk, satin, taffeta and very heavily glazed cotton are also unsuitable. They tend to fray too easily, pucker when sewn together and do not stuff well. Cotton prints are often considerably improved if they are washed before use, to remove the dressing. Very loosely woven materials such as some mohair tweeds, velvet and fur fabrics are rather more difficult to handle successfully and are therefore not recommended for use by beginners. When some skill has been acquired in manipulating materials, then these materials can be used to make very attractive toys indeed.

Patchwork bundles containing a selection of small pieces of various materials can be obtained at a reasonable cost. These bundles can be very useful if several toys are to be made or to start a bit-bag.

Small pieces of felt are required for most of the toys. They can be obtained in a variety of sizes from a 150 mm (6 in.) square to a 910 mm (36 in.) square or bought by the yard if larger quantities are required. Felt is usually obtainable from most large departmental stores and from needlework or craft shops. (See suppliers' list.)

If the toys are to be washed it is necessary to shrink the felt first before cutting out the pieces. This is done by ironing the felt over a damp cloth.

Knitting wool is required for some of the toys, both double knitting and very thick wool (double double knitting wool). The wool must be in hanks so that it can be laid out flat and cut into the required lengths. To make a hank from a ball of wool, wind the wool round the back of an easy chair. Rinse the wool in warm water and hang up to dry to remove all the crinkles from the wool.

Tools and materials

Paper or thin card for making the patterns. Graph paper is most suitable
Large envelopes in which to keep the patterns
Pencil
Tailor's chalk
Compass
Set square or a piece of card with a right angle such as the lid of a box
Ruler
Tape measure
Scissors for cutting out paper
Scissors for cutting materials
Small scissors
Assorted sewing cottons
Button thread
Black embroidery thread
Assorted needles, including a large tapestry needle or a bodkin.
Blunt knitting needle or wooden stick for stuffing
Pins
Glue, either white or transparent
Wire brush
Raffia or cellophane string for whiskers
Hardboard for the base of the pouffes.

Cutting out the pattern pieces

This is a very important process and care taken at this stage will be rewarded later on. Bad cutting results in misshapen toys and pattern pieces that do not fit together properly. It is essential to use a very sharp pair of scissors for cutting out materials and another pair for cutting paper or cardboard. Never use the same pair for both processes as the paper ruins the cutting edge of the scissors. Felt pieces for details such as eyes must be cut with a continuous action, not a series of short, jagged cuts. See diagram illustrating this point.

Place the material to be cut out on a table with the wrong side uppermost. Arrange the patterns as economically as possible on the material, making sure that the selvedge runs in the same direction as the arrows marked on the patterns. When using pile fabrics such as velvet, blanketing and fur fabrics, stroke the material first to see which way the pile lies and then place the patterns on the material with the arrows

10

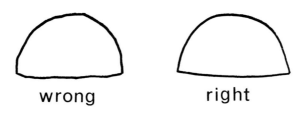

wrong right

pointing in the same direction. When using materials which have a right and wrong side, for example pile fabrics and printed fabrics, remember to reverse any pattern which is asymmetrical and which requires more than one piece to be cut from the pattern. See diagram. This does not apply to materials such as felt, sheeting or similar reversible materials.

To obtain a perfect match when using striped or large patterned materials it may be necessary to lay the patterns on the right side of the material.

If paper patterns are used, pin these carefully to the material using plenty of pins. Then cut exactly round the edge of each pattern. If cardboard patterns are used, place these on the material and weight them in the middle with a heavy object. Draw round each pattern using tailor's chalk on dark materials and a pencil or a laundry marking pen on lighter coloured materials. Keep both the pencil and tailor's chalk very sharp

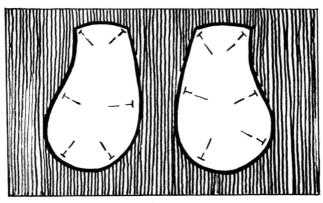

reversing the pattern

so that a thin, clean line appears on the material. Never use a ballpoint or fibre-tipped pens as they tend to smudge. Cut out each pattern carefully following the outline.

Sewing the pattern pieces together

This process may be done by hand sewing, using a double length of thread, or by machine stitching. Choose a sewing cotton that matches the colour of the materials selected. This is particularly important when attaching ears and other details, where the stitching is more likely to be seen. If the children's pouffés are to be sewn together by hand it is essential to use a strong button thread as there is so much pressure on the seams. If they are to be sewn by machine, then work two rows of machine stitching along each seam for extra strength.

It is recommended that beginners tack the pieces together before commencing to sew. It is advisable not to use pins as these could possibly be left in the toy. Tacking is also suggested when using fur fabrics and striped or patterned materials which are to be matched. Unless you are experienced on a sewing machine, it would be preferable to stitch the toys by hand using back stitch. It is, however, an advantage to machine stitch the children's pouffes as these are so much larger than the other toys and the seams must be very strong to withstand the pressure of a child's weight. If the sewing machine has a lever for reversing the stitch, this is very useful, particularly on either side of the opening which has been left for turning and stuffing. The reverse stitching prevents the seam from coming undone while the stuffing is being pushed into the toy. There is a considerable strain at this point, so hand sewers must finish off each thread very securely. The protruding edge of pile on fur fabrics must be tucked into the seam, using a needle to poke it in before stitching the seam together. If this is done carefully the seams should be hardly visible on the right side.

Place all the pattern pieces together with right sides facing unless otherwise stated in the individual instructions. Follow the instructions given for each toy. Carefully match the letters marked on the patterns and snip the seams at all points marked by a black triangle. To ensure that all the pattern pieces fit together properly, keep all the stitching 6 mm ($\frac{1}{4}$ in.) away from the edge for the smaller toys and 13 mm ($\frac{1}{2}$ in.) away for the children's pouffes.

Stuffing the toy

This is also a very important process and should be done slowly and carefully. The amount of stuffing used and the way that it is put into the toy, determines the final shape. It is not possible to rearrange the stuffing once the main part of the body has been stuffed. The only way to improve on weak points is to take all the stuffing out and to start over again.

Pure kapok is the best type of stuffing for most toys, although it is slightly more expensive and does not wash quite as well as some other stuffing materials. It has the advantage of moulding very well, is light and clean and is fairly quickly packed into a toy. Kapok mixtures, foam chips and even old, clean nylon stockings are all quite suitable. Foam chips are often only available in colours and are therefore unsuitable for stuffing white or pale coloured materials as the coloured pieces may show through. Foam chips and nylon stockings have the advantage of drying very quickly. If the toy is likely to require frequent washing, these materials would be preferable, although they take a long time to put into a toy. Cotton wool and other cotton flock mixtures, which are cheaper than pure kapok, are not suitable for the narrow parts of toys as the stuffing tends to form into hard lumps. If economy is important, it is possible to stuff the narrow parts with kapok and then to finish the main parts with cotton flock.

The children's pouffes require a combination of kapok or cotton flock and wood wool. There are several different grades of wood wool and it is only sold in very large quantities. It is, however, used for packing such things as china and glass and many china shops are willing to give it away. Choose the finest grade that is available as this is much easier to stuff than the coarser grades.

Always stuff the extremities of a toy first, starting with very small quantities. Use a stuffing stick, the blunt end of a pencil or steel knitting needle to help push the stuffing into difficult corners. Continue putting small quantities into the toy, pressing them in evenly and tightly to avoid a lumpy effect, until the main body part is reached. It is now possible to speed up the process by putting the stuffing into the toy in handfuls, still pressing tightly and firmly and moulding the toy to the required shape.

It is better to have a toy that is stuffed too hard than too soft. If too soft, it will soon develop a wobbly head and floppy arms and legs when in use. The children's pouffes must be stuffed as hard as possible or they soon lose their shape. It needs a man's strength to make a really successful pouffe, so if you can enlist some help, your toy will retain it's shape much longer. It is preferable to line the head with a layer of kapok or cotton flock before packing in the wood wool. This makes the toy feel soft and prevents small pieces of the wood wool working their way through the material. The wood wool must be loose when put into the pouffe. If it has solid lumps or tangles, these must be teased out before it is usable.

As wood wool is a very dusty material, it is advisable to do the stuffing outside if possible. Failing this, cover yourself and the floor completely before commencing to stuff.

Pack the wood wool into the toy as hard as possible, using a stick or wooden spoon. An overall is advised when using any kind of stuffing as it tends to cling to everything and can be difficult to remove, from woollen garments particularly. A wire brush is the most effective way of removing surplus stuffing from the toy and from chairs and carpets.

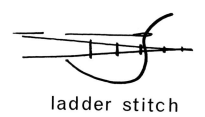

ladder stitch

When the stuffing is completed, sew up the opening using ladder stitch and button thread. See diagram. This stitch turns in the two raw edges as it is being worked and when it is pulled tightly together should give an invisible join. It is also a useful stitch for attaching arms, legs, etc to the body. Remove any remains of the stuffing from the toy with a small wire brush. If any fur pile has become embedded in the seams, poke this out with a small knitting needle so that the seams are almost invisible.

Finishing details

The positioning of details such as eyes and ears will give each toy an individual character. By moving them just slightly the expression of the toy can be completely altered. Using the positions marked on the patterns as a guide, experiment with the placing of the features, moving them about until the most appealing expression is obtained. Make sure that these additional parts are very firmly attached to the toy, as they are usually the first things that small children attempt to remove! Felt pieces have been used for all the toys' eyes because mothers are very critical of glass eyes, which could come off and be swallowed by children. It would be quite permissible, however, to use buttons, beads or glass eyes on older children's toys provided they are sewn on very securely and preferably glued as well. Glass eyes for toys are sold in pairs in various sizes and colours.

The toys have been designed so that there are as few additional pieces as possible to sew on after the toy has been stuffed. Many of the toys have their manes, tails, ears, etc actually sewn in to the seams. This both saves time and ensures that they are securely attached to the body and have a neater appearance. Do not judge your toy too harshly until it is finally completed. None of the toys look attractive until all the details are finished and the toy has a personality.

Fish

Materials

460 mm ($\frac{1}{2}$ yd) of printed cotton towelling, corduroy or furnishing fabric. Choose a brightly coloured abstract or floral design in blues and greens for the body. This toy is a simple shape with very little embellishment, relying on the attractiveness of the material selected for success.
A small piece of pink or red felt for the mouth
A small piece of white felt for the eyes
A small piece of black or coloured felt for the eyeballs
A 230 mm (9 in.) square of a bright coloured felt for the tail, gills and fin
    If preferred these three patterns can be cut from different coloured felts, in which case a small quantity of each is required.
Either transparent or white glue
Stuffing approximately 320 grammes (11 oz).

To cut out

Make the paper patterns, using the diagram in which one square equals 20 mm ($\frac{3}{4}$ in.) as a guide. This size produces a toy 305 mm (12 in.) from nose to tail. Cut the pattern pieces as follows:
Body   cut two in printed cotton material
Body Gusset   cut one in printed cotton material
Eye   cut two in white felt
Eyeball   cut two in black or coloured felt
Mouth   cut one in red or pink felt
Tail   cut two in a brightly coloured felt
Gill   cut two in a bright felt
Fin   cut one in a bright felt.

16

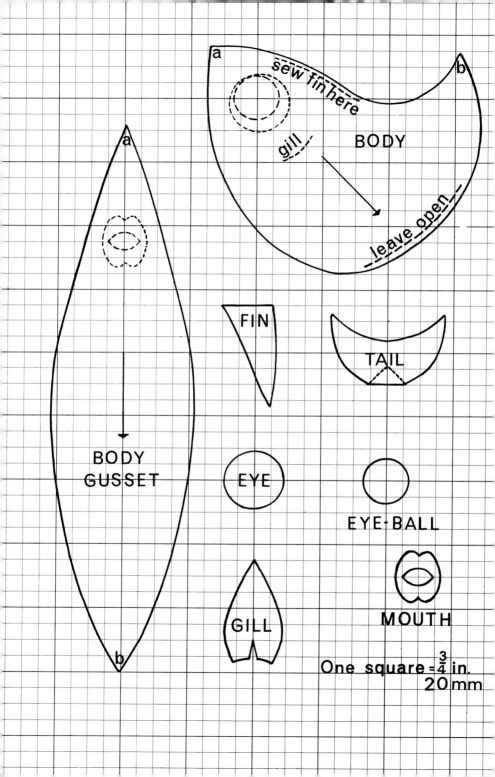

a

b

sew fin here

gill

BODY

leave open

a

BODY
GUSSET

FIN

TAIL

EYE

EYE-BALL

GILL

MOUTH

b

One square = $\frac{3}{4}$ in.
20 mm

To make up

Sew the darts together on the two felt gills. Open out and press each one. Sew each gill to each body piece in the position marked on the pattern with the wrong side of the gill to the right side of the body. Tack the fin to one body piece in the position marked on the pattern and close to the edge. Place the two body pieces together with right sides facing. Sew from A to B, sewing through the fin at the same time. Place one side of the body gusset to one side of the body; sew from A to B with right sides facing. Repeat for the other side but leave an opening of approximately 102 mm (4 in.) in the position indicated by the dotted line on the body pattern. Turn to the right side and stuff fairly firmly. Sew up the opening with ladder stitch. Sew the two tail pieces together close to the edge, leaving the straight edge open. Sew together along the dotted line marked on the tail pattern. Place the tail over point B and sew securely to the body. Glue the eyeballs to the eyes and then glue the eyes to the body in the position marked on the pattern. Glue the mouth to the body gusset in the position marked on the pattern.

Dachshund

Materials

685 mm ($\frac{3}{4}$ yd) of printed dress or furnishing fabric. A striped pattern in multi-colours makes a very attractive toy
A small piece of black felt for the nose and eyeballs
A small piece of white or coloured felt for the eyes
Either transparent or white glue
Stuffing approximately 340 grammes (12 oz).

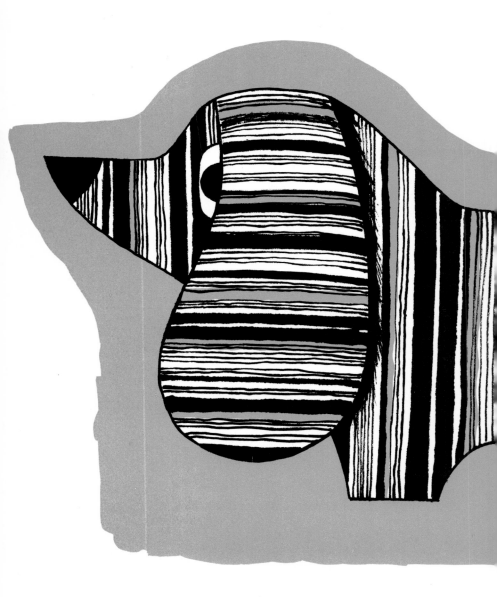

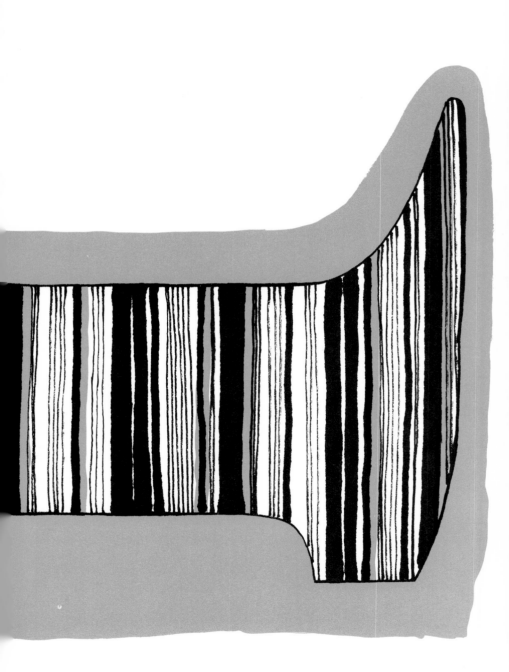

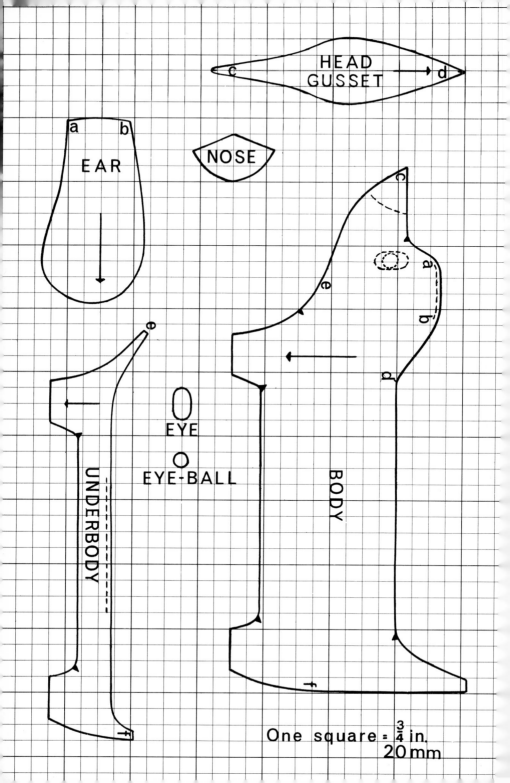

HEAD GUSSET

c ──► d

EAR

a   b

NOSE

BODY

c

a

b

d

e

UNDERBODY

e

EYE

EYE-BALL

f

One square = ¾ in.
20 mm

To cut out

Make the paper patterns, using the diagram in which one square equals 20 mm ($\frac{3}{4}$ in.) as a guide. This size produces a toy 560 mm (22 in.) from nose to tail. Cut the pattern pieces as follows:

Body   cut two in printed fabric
Underbody   cut two in printed fabric
Ear   cut four in printed fabric
Head gusset   cut one in printed fabric
Nose   cut one in black felt
Eyeball   cut two in black felt
Eye   cut two in white or coloured felt.

To make up

Place each pair of ears together, right sides facing and sew round, leaving the top edge open. Turn to the right side and press the ears. Sew an ear to each body piece with right sides facing 3 mm ($\frac{1}{8}$ in.) from the edge, matching A to A and B to B. Sew the head gusset to each body piece with right sides facing, matching C to C and D to D. Make sure that the stitching of the ears to the body is completely covered.

Place the two underbody pieces together with right sides facing. Sew from E to F, leaving an opening of approximately 100 mm (4 in.) in the centre of the seam as indicated by the dotted line on the pattern. Sew each underbody piece to each body piece with right sides facing from E round the legs to F. Complete the body by sewing from D to F and E to C. Snip at all the triangular marks on the pattern to ease the seam, taking care not to cut the stitching. Turn to the right side and stuff very firmly. Sew up the opening with ladder stitch.

Fold the felt piece for the nose in half and sew the two straight edges together. Turn to the right side, place over the nose on the body and slip stitch into position. Glue the eyeballs to the eyes and then glue to the head in the position indicated on the pattern.

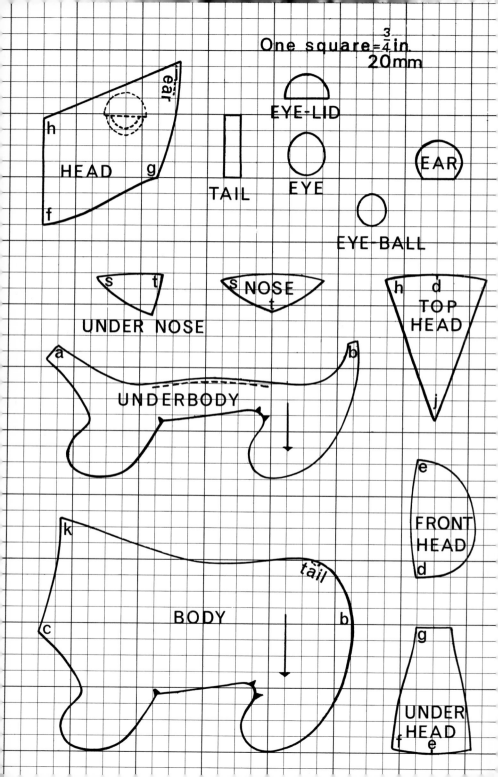

Lion

Materials

300 mm ($\frac{1}{3}$ yd) of printed dress or furnishing fabric for the body. The head requires three different coloured felts: a light colour for the front of the head, a medium tone for the head and underhead, and a darker colour for the top of the head, in the following quantities:

A 230 mm (9 in.) square for the top of the head, ears and tail
A 300 mm (12 in.) square for the head and underhead
A 150 mm (6 in.) square for the front of the head
A small piece of black felt for the nose and eyeballs
A small piece of felt for the eyelids
A small piece of white felt for the eyes
Black embroidery thread
A 100 mm (4 in.) length of cord for the tail
A 60 grammes (2 oz) hank or ball of brown chunky knit wool for the mane and tail
Either transparent or white glue
Stuffing approximately 340 grammes (12 oz).

To cut out

Make the paper patterns, using the diagram as a guide in which one square equals 20 mm ($\frac{3}{4}$ in.). This size produces a toy 480 mm (19 in.) from nose to tail.

Cut the pattern pieces as follows:

Body   cut two in printed material
Underbody   cut two in printed material
Head   cut two in a medium toned felt
Underhead   cut one in a medium toned felt
Front Head   cut two in a light coloured felt
Top Head   cut one in a darker felt
Ear   cut four in a darker felt
Tail   cut one in a darker felt
Nose   cut one in black felt
Undernose   cut two in black felt
Eyeball   cut two in black felt
Eye   cut two in white felt
Eyelid   cut two in fawn or brown felt.

To make up

Place the two underbody pieces together with right sides facing. Sew from A to B, leaving an opening of approximately

100 mm (4 in.) in the centre of the seam as indicated by the dotted line on the pattern. Sew one side of the underbody to one body piece with right sides facing from C round the legs to B.

Sew the two front head pieces together from D to E. Sew the underhead to each side of the head pieces, matching F to F and G to G. Sew the top head piece to each side of the head pieces, matching H to H and J to J. Insert the front head piece and sew to the rest of the head, matching D to D and E to E. Turn to the right side.

Sew each pair of ears together, leaving the straight edge open. Turn to the right side. Gather slightly across the bottom and sew to each side of the head about 25 mm (1 in.) away from point J as indicated on the pattern.

Fold the strip of felt for the tail round the 100 (4 in.) length of cord and oversew together. Gather one end slightly. Cut a 100 mm (4 in.) length of wool from the hank of chunky knit wool, fold it in half and sew it securely to the gathered end of the tail. Trim the wool if required.

Using the remainder of the hank of wool, cut it into equal lengths approximately 200 mm (8 in.) long. Fold each length in half and place side by side along the neck edge of the body, leaving 6 mm ($\frac{1}{4}$ in.) uncovered at each end. The cut ends of the wool should be placed to the raw edge of the material and the wool carefully arranged so that it covers evenly. Tack the wool into position and then sew securely to the body. It is preferable to machine stitch the wool to the body as this ensures that all the strands of wool are securely attached and will not pull out when the toy is in use.

Sew the two undernose pieces together along the short edge. Open out and with right sides facing, sew to the nose piece, matching S to S and T to T.

Complete the body by sewing from K to B. Place the head inside the body with right sides facing and sew together, matching J to K and G to C. Use strong thread for this seam. Turn to the right side and stuff firmly. Sew up the opening with ladder stitch.

Place some stuffing on the inside of the nose and sew to the head, matching S to H. Sew the tail to the body very securely in the position indicated on the pattern. Work a row of chain stitch in black embroidery thread as shown on the illustration. Glue the eyeballs and eyelids to the eyes. Then glue to the head in the position shown on the pattern.

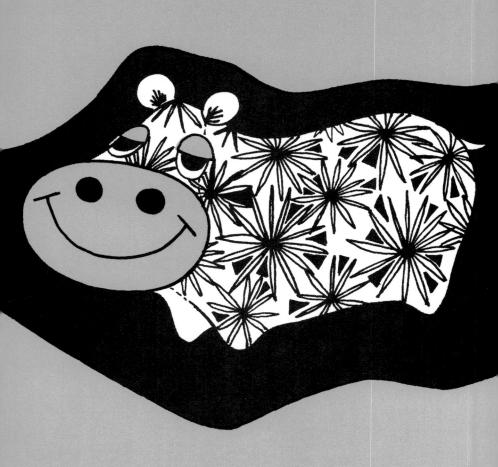

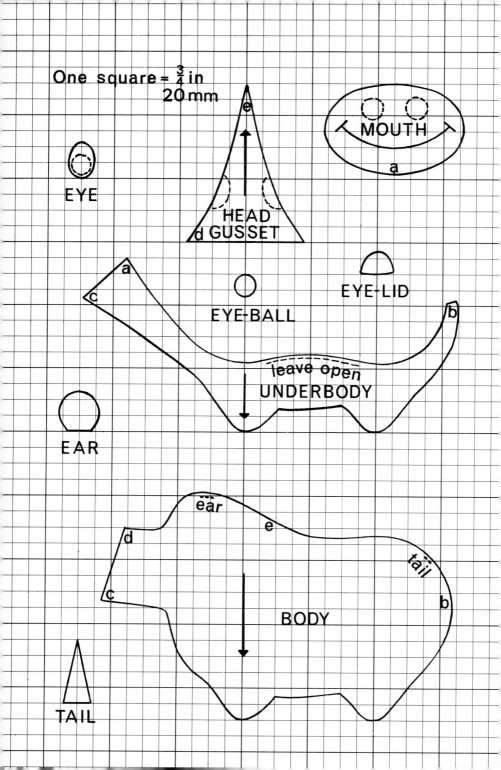

One square = $\frac{3}{4}$ in
20 mm

EYE

HEAD
d GUSSET

e

MOUTH
a

EYE-LID

EYE-BALL

a

c

b

leave open
UNDERBODY

EAR

ear

d

e

tail

c

b

BODY

TAIL

Hippopotamus

Materials

460 mm ($\frac{1}{2}$ yd) of cotton material printed with a small floral design, printed towelling or corduroy for the body
A 230 mm (9 in.) square of felt for the mouth and tail, choose a colour which complements the body material or which matches one of the colours in the printed design
A small piece of white felt for the eyes
A small piece of black felt for the eyeballs
A small piece of coloured felt for the eyelids
A small piece of coloured felt for the nostrils
685 mm ($\frac{3}{4}$ yd) of ribbon
Black embroidery thread for the mouth
Either transparent or white glue
Stuffing approximately 340 grammes (12 oz).

To cut out

Make the paper patterns, using the diagram in which one square equals 20 mm ($\frac{3}{4}$ in.) as a guide. This size of square produces a toy approximately 380 mm (15 in.) long from nose to tail. Cut the pattern pieces as follows:
Body   cut two in printed material
Underbody   cut two in printed material
Head Gusset   cut one in printed material
Ear   cut four in printed material
Mouth   cut one in felt
Tail   cut two in felt
Eye   cut two in white felt
Eyeball   cut two in black felt
Eyelid   cut two in felt
Eyeball   cut two in coloured felt for the nostrils

To make up

Sew the two underbody pieces together with right sides facing from A to B, leaving an opening of about 100 mm (4 in.) in the centre as indicated by the dotted line on the pattern. Sew each side of the underbody to each body piece with right sides facing, matching B to B and C to C.

Sew each pair of ears together leaving the straight edge open. Turn each ear to the right side. Sew the head gusset to each side of the body with right sides facing and matching D to D and E to E, inserting the ears at the same time in the position marked on the body pattern. Sew the two body pieces together along the back from E to B.

With right sides facing sew the felt piece for the mouth to the body, matching A to A. Turn the completed body to the right side and stuff firmly. Sew up the opening.

Oversew the two felt pieces for the tail together all the way round, then sew securely to the back of the body. Work a row of stitching for the mouth using black embroidery thread and glue on the nostrils in the position indicated on the pattern. Glue the eyeballs to the eyes and then glue to the head in the position indicated on the head gusset pattern. Glue the eyelids over the top half of the eyes. Finally tie a length of ribbon round the neck of the hippopotamus.

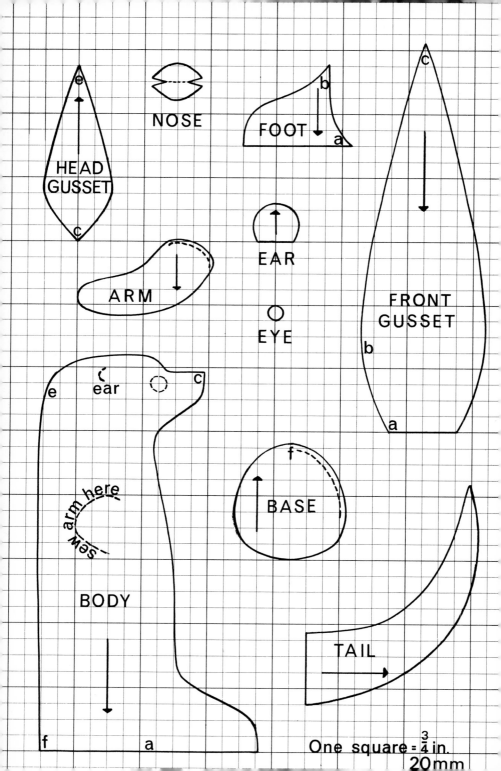

NOSE

HEAD GUSSET

FOOT

e

c

b

a

EAR

EYE

ARM

c

FRONT GUSSET

b

a

e

ear

c

f

BASE

sew arm here

BODY

TAIL

f

a

One square = $\frac{3}{4}$ in.
20mm

Otter

Materials

460 mm ($\frac{1}{2}$ yd) of grey, green or brown fur fabric for the body. The same quantity of an interesting tweed in these colours may be used as an alternative.
A piece of white fur fabric 460 mm × 150 mm (18 in. × 6 in.) with the pile running vertically for the front body. Velvet or blanketing may be used as an alternative if preferred
A small piece of black felt for the nose and eyes
A 230 mm (9 in.) length of raffia or cellophane string for the whiskers
Either transparent or white glue
Stuffing approximately 400 grammes (14 oz).

To cut out

Make the paper patterns, using the diagram in which one square equals 20 mm ($\frac{3}{4}$ in.) as a guide. This size produces a toy 460 mm (18 in.) high. Cut the pattern pieces as follows:
Body   cut two in fur fabric or tweed
Tail   cut two in fur fabric or tweed
Arm   cut four in fur fabric or tweed
Foot   cut two in fur fabric or tweed
Ear   cut four in fur fabric or tweed
Head Gusset   cut one in fur fabric or tweed
Base   cut one in fur fabric or tweed
Front Gusset   cut one in white fur fabric or velvet or blanketing
Nose   cut one in black felt
Eye   cut two in black felt.

To make up

Sew the two pieces for the feet on either side of the front gusset with right sides facing, matching A to A and B to B. Tack the front gusset and feet to each body piece with right sides facing, matching C to C and A to A. Then sew together. Tack the head gusset to each side of the body with right sides facing, matching C to C and E to E. Sew together. Sew the two body pieces together down the back from E to F. Tack the base to the bottom of the body with right sides facing, matching F to F. Sew together leaving an opening of approximately 100 mm (4 in.) on one side as indicated by the dotted line on the pattern. Turn to the right side and stuff fairly firmly. Sew up the opening with ladder stitch.

Sew the two tail pieces together with right sides facing, leaving the straight edge open. Trim the point. Then turn to the right side and stuff. Turn in the raw edges and tack. Sew the tail to the back of the body with the tail lying horizontally, using button thread to make sure it is securely attached.

Sew each pair of ears together with right sides facing, leaving the straight edge open. Turn to the right side. Turn in the raw edges and oversew together, using button thread, and gathering slightly at the same time. Sew securely to the head in the position marked on the pattern.

Sew each pair of arms together with right sides facing. Leave the wider end open as indicated by the dotted line on the pattern. Turn to the right side and stuff. Sew up the opening with ladder stitch. Then sew securely to each side of the body in the position indicated on the pattern, using button thread.

Fold the felt piece for the nose in half along the dotted line marked on the pattern and oversew the straight edges together. Turn to the right side. Put a little stuffing in the nose and then sew to the head.

Make a knot about 50 mm (2 in.) from the end of the 230 mm (9 in.) length of raffia or cellophane string. Thread the raffia or string in a bodkin and pull through the head on either side of the nose. Make another knot on the other side as close to the head as possible. Then trim the ends of the raffia or string and fray them out to make the whiskers. It may be necessary to use pliers to get the raffia through the head.

Glue the eyes to the head in the position marked on the pattern.

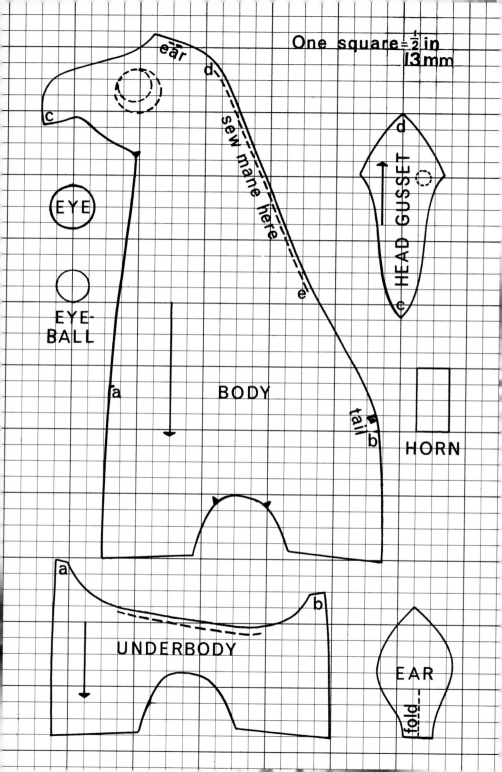

Giraffe

Materials

460 mm ($\frac{1}{2}$ yd) of printed cotton, towelling or printed furnishing fabric for the body
A strip of dark coloured felt 50 mm × 200 mm (2 in. × 8 in.) for the mane
A 150 mm (6 in.) square of felt for the horns and ears, the same colour as the mane or an alternative colour
A small piece of white felt for the eyes and a small piece of black felt for the eyeballs
A 150 mm (6 in.) length of furnishing cord for the tail
Either transparent or white glue
Stuffing approximately 200 grammes (8 oz).

To cut out

Make the paper patterns, using the diagram in which one square equals 13 mm ($\frac{1}{2}$ in.) as a guide. This size produces a toy 410 mm (16 in.) high. Cut the pattern pieces as follows:
Body   cut two in printed fabric
Underbody   cut two in printed fabric
Head Gusset   cut one in printed fabric
Ear   cut two in black or a dark coloured felt
Horn   cut two in black or a dark coloured felt
Mane   cut one 50 mm × 200 mm (2 in. × 8 in.) strip of black or dark coloured felt
Eye   cut two in white felt
Eyeball   cut two in black felt.

To make up

Fold each ear in half along the dotted line marked on the pattern. Sew together across the straight edge and for 13 mm ($\frac{1}{2}$ in.) up the side. Fold the 50 mm × 200 mm (2 in. × 8 in.) felt strip for the mane in half lengthwise and make a series of cuts, starting from the folded edge and finishing 6 mm ($\frac{1}{4}$ in.) from the cut edges. The cuts should be approximately 6 mm ($\frac{1}{4}$ in.) apart and continue the whole length of the strip. Sew the two cut edges together.

Place the two underbody pieces together with right sides facing. Sew from A to B, leaving an opening of approximately 90 mm ($3\frac{1}{2}$ in.) as indicated by the dotted line on the underbody pattern. Sew one side of the underbody to one body piece with right sides facing from A round the legs to B. Repeat for the other side. Snip at the points marked on the pattern, taking care not to cut the stitching.

Sew the head gusset to one side of the body piece with right sides facing, matching C to C and D to D. At the same time insert the ear into this seam in the position marked on the pattern. Repeat for the other side. Insert the 200 mm (8 in.) strip of fringed felt between the two body pieces, commencing at point D and finishing at point E. Tack these three layers together close to the edge. Then sew from D to B, inserting the cord for the tail just before point B. Knot one end of the cord and make sure that it is stitched to the body very securely. Sew together the front of the body from A to C. Turn the completed body to the right side and stuff firmly. Sew up the opening with ladder stitch.

Make a tight roll from each of the pieces of felt for the horns. Slipstitch or glue the edge to prevent them from unwinding. Sew each horn very securely to the top of the head as indicated by the small circle on the head gusset pattern. Glue the eyeballs to the eyes and then glue to each side of the head in the position indicated on the body pattern.

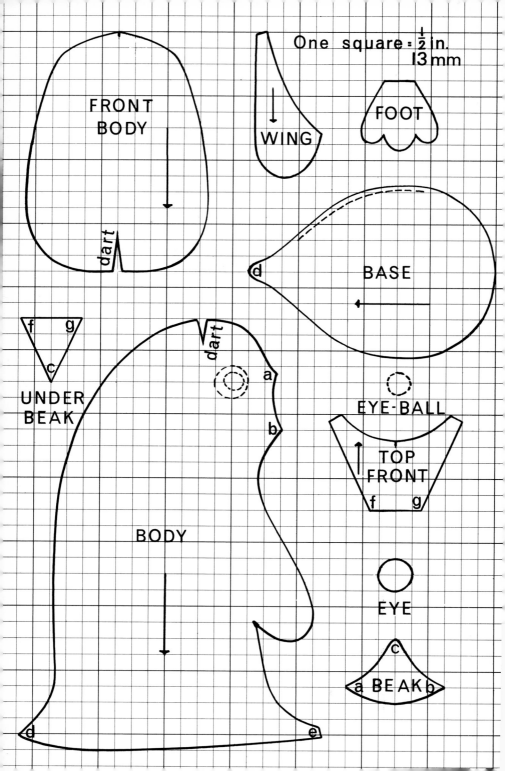

One square = ½ in.
13 mm

FRONT BODY

dart

WING

FOOT

BASE

d

UNDER BEAK

f g

c

BODY

dart

a

b

EYE-BALL

TOP FRONT

f g

EYE

d

e

c

a BEAK b

Penguin

Materials

A piece of white fur fabric 150 mm × 200 mm (6 in. × 8 in.) for the front body
460 mm ($\frac{1}{2}$ yd) of black fur fabric 1220 mm (48 in.) wide for the body. This quantity is sufficient for two penguins
A 230 mm (9 in.) square of orange or yellow felt for the beak and feet
A small piece of white felt for the eyes
A small piece of black felt for the eyeballs
Either transparent or white glue
Stuffing approximately 200 grammes (7 oz).

To cut out

Make the paper patterns, using the diagram in which one square equals 13 mm ($\frac{1}{2}$ in.) as a guide. This size produces a toy 300 mm (12 in.) high. Cut the pattern pieces as follows:
Body   cut two in black fur fabric
Front Body   cut one in white fur fabric
Base   cut one in black fur fabric
Wing   cut two in black fur fabric
Top Front   cut one in black fur fabric
Beak   cut two in orange or yellow felt
Underbeak   cut one in orange or yellow felt
Foot   cut four in orange or yellow felt
Eye   cut two in white felt
Eyeball   cut two in black felt.

To make up

Sew each dart together at the top of the two body pieces. Sew each beak piece to each body piece, matching A to A and B to B and with right sides facing. Place the two body pieces together with right sides facing and sew from C to D. Sew the body pieces together with right sides facing across the short edge at point E.

Sew the short end of each wing to the two short edges on the top front piece with right sides facing. Fold the top front piece in half and mark the centre point on the curved edge with a pin. Fold the front body piece in half and mark the top centre point in the same way. Pin the top front to the front body piece, matching the two centre points and with right sides facing. Tack the top front and the wings to the front body. Then sew together.

Sew the under beak to the top front piece, matching F to F and G to G, with right sides facing. Sew the dart together at the bottom of the front body.

Tack the front body, wings and beak to the body pieces with right sides facing. Take care that the dart on the front body is positioned at point E. Sew the two pieces together right round. Snip under the arm to ease the seam, taking care not to cut the stitching.

Tack the base to the bottom of the body, matching D to D and with right sides facing. Leave an opening of approximately 100 mm (4 in.) on one side as indicated by the dotted line on the base pattern. Turn to the right ride and stuff fairly firmly, making sure that there is sufficient stuffing in the beak and wings. Sew up the opening with ladder stitch.

Sew each pair of feet together 3 mm ($\frac{1}{8}$ in.) from the edge, leaving the straight edge open. Stuff lightly and then oversew the open edges together. Sew the feet to the front of the body very securely approximately 20 mm ($\frac{3}{4}$ in.) from either side of the dart.

Glue or sew the eyeballs to the eyes. Then glue or sew to the head in the position indicated on the pattern.

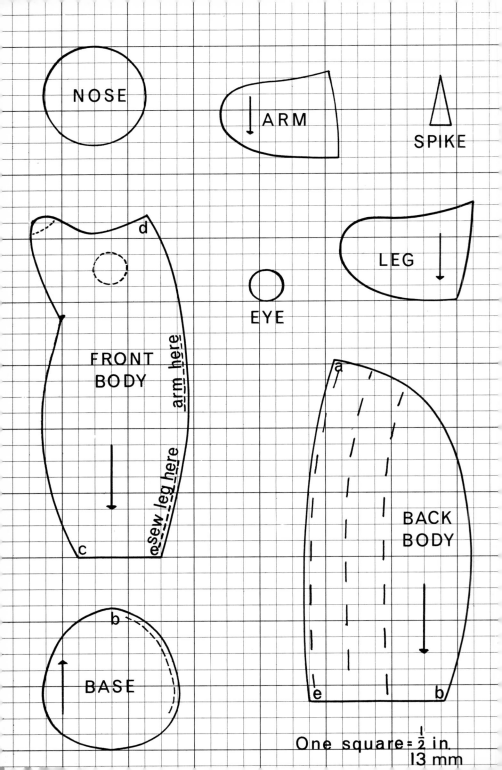

Hedgehog

Materials

230 mm ($\frac{1}{4}$ yd) of self-coloured towelling, velvet or woollen material for the front body. It is preferable to choose a light colour for this and a darker colour for the back of the body.
300 mm ($\frac{1}{3}$ yd) of mohair, bouclé or any other interesting tweed for the back of the body and the arms and legs
A 300 mm (12 in.) square of black felt for the nose, eyes and spikes
Either transparent or white glue
Stuffing approximately 170 grammes (6 oz).

To cut out

Make the paper patterns, using the diagram in which one square equals 13 mm ($\frac{1}{2}$ in.) as a guide. This size produces a toy 240 mm ($9\frac{1}{2}$ in.) high. Cut the pattern pieces as follows:
Front Body   cut two in self-coloured material
Back Body   cut two in tweed
Base   cut one in tweed
Leg   cut four in tweed
Arm   cut four in tweed
Nose   cut one in black felt
Eye   cut two in black felt
Spike   cut approximately thirty-two in black or coloured felt if preferred.

To make up

Place the two back body pieces together with right sides facing. Sew from A to B. Open out these two pieces and turn to the right side. Pin or tack three rows of felt spikes to the back body commencing 6 mm ($\frac{1}{4}$ in.) from the raw edge leaving approximately 25 mm (1 in.) between each spike. On the second and third rows the spikes should be placed so that they fill the spaces left in the previous row as indicated on the body pattern. If desired, the spikes may be machined to the body in lines. This is obviously much quicker than hand sewing, but does not give quite such a neat appearance. Keep three or four spikes to sew over the back seam when the toy has been stuffed.

Place the two front body pieces together with right sides facing. Sew from C to D. Sew each pair of legs together with right sides facing, leaving the short edges open. Turn to the right side and stuff lightly. Repeat this process for the arms. Sew the legs and arms to each side of the front body in the positions marked on the pattern and with right sides facing. Sew the front body to the back body with right sides facing, matching E to E and A to D.

Insert the base at the bottom of the front and back body, with right sides facing. Sew together, matching B to B and leaving an opening on one side as indicated by the dotted line on the base pattern. Turn to the right side and stuff. Sew up the opening with ladder stitch. Sew the remaining three or four spikes over the back seam. Work a gathering thread round the black felt circle for the nose, close to the edge. Pull the thread fairly tight and stuff lightly. Sew securely to the nose on the body. Glue on the eyes in the position indicated on the pattern.

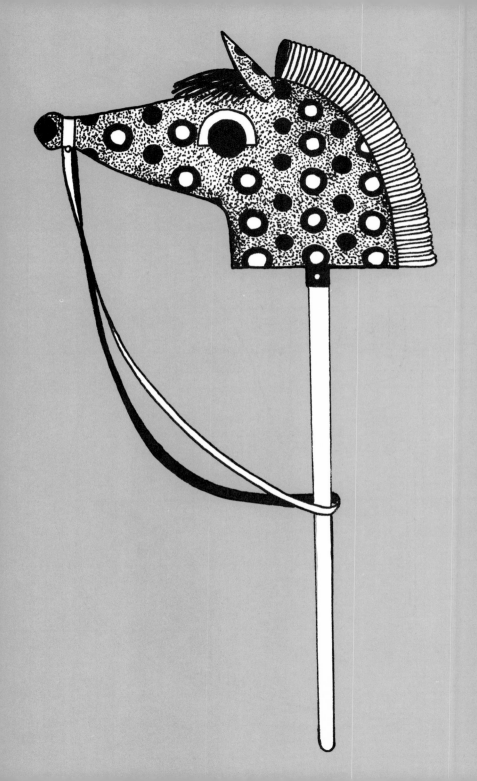

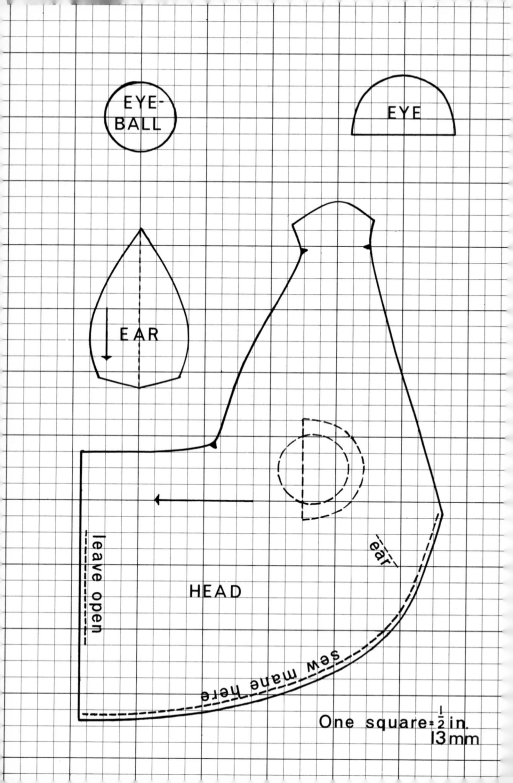

EYE-BALL

EYE

EAR

leave open

HEAD

ear

sew mane here

One square = $\frac{1}{2}$ in.
13 mm

Hobby horse

Materials

300 mm ($\frac{1}{3}$ yd) of strong cotton or woollen material for the head and ears
A small piece of stiffening material for the ears
A strip of felt 100 mm × 38 mm (4 in. × 1$\frac{1}{2}$ in.) for the top of the pole
A small piece of white or coloured felt for the eyes
A small piece of black felt for the eyeballs
28 grammes (1 oz) hank of double knitting wool for the mane
Stuffing approximately 230 grammes (8 oz)
Either transparent or white glue
460 mm (1$\frac{1}{2}$ yds) of carpet tape, ribbon or leather approximately 25 mm (1 in.) wide for the reins
A brush handle or dowelling 25 mm (1 in.) diameter and 910 mm (36 in.) long, for the pole
A small quantity of enamel in a bright colour if the pole is to be painted
Two of each of the following: carpet tacks, brass upholstery studs, brass eyelets and bells.

To cut out

Make the paper patterns, using the diagram in which one square equals 13 mm ($\frac{1}{2}$ in.) as a guide. This size produces a toy 100 mm (41 in.) high. Cut the pattern pieces as follows:
Head   cut two in strong cotton or woollen material
Ear   cut four in strong cotton or woollen material and two in a stiffening material
Eye   cut two in white or coloured felt
Eyeball   cut two in black felt.

To make up

Cut the hank of double knitting wool in half. Then cut it into 130 mm (5 in.) lengths. Fold all these lengths in half. Lay them side by side along the right side of one of the head pieces in the position marked on the pattern, with the folded edge to the inside. Tack and then sew the wool to the head piece. Sew the two head pieces together with right sides facing, leaving an opening of approximately 100 mm (4 in.) along the bottom straight edge as indicated on the pattern. Snip the seam at the triangular marks, taking care not to cut the stitching. Turn to the right side and stuff very firmly, leaving a space up the middle to accommodate the pole.

The pole looks more attractive if it is painted a bright colour. If it is to be left plain, a coat of varnish would help to keep it looking clean and new. Make sure that either paint or varnish is thoroughly dry before pushing into the head. Put some glue on the top 100 mm (4 in.) of the pole. Then push into the head keeping it central and vertical. Finish stuffing and sew up the opening on either side of the pole, using ladder stitch. Attach the remaining raw edges to the pole with a carpet tack on either side. Cover the tacks by gluing the felt strip round the top of the pole. Secure with two brass upholstery studs, one on each side.

Place each pair of ears together with right sides facing. Then place one piece of stiffening on top of each. Sew all three layers together, leaving the straight edges open. Trim the point and then turn to the right side. Turn in the raw edges and oversew together. Fold each ear in half and oversew together. Sew very securely to the head in the position indicated on the pattern.

Cut through the first loop of wool at the top of the head to make the forelock. Glue the eyeballs to the eyes and then glue to each side of the head in the position marked on the pattern.

If carpet tape is used for the reins, this must be folded in half lengthwise. The two self-adhesive sides will stick together to give a 25 mm (1 in.) wide strip. Join the length of carpet tape, ribbon or leather together. A brass eyelet gives the most professional result, but sewing or gluing are quite adequate. Fold the reins in half with the join at one end. Then, using the other end, place over the nose at the narrowest point and secure underneath either by sewing or with a brass eyelet. Sew or tie a pair of bells to the reins, as near to the head as possible.

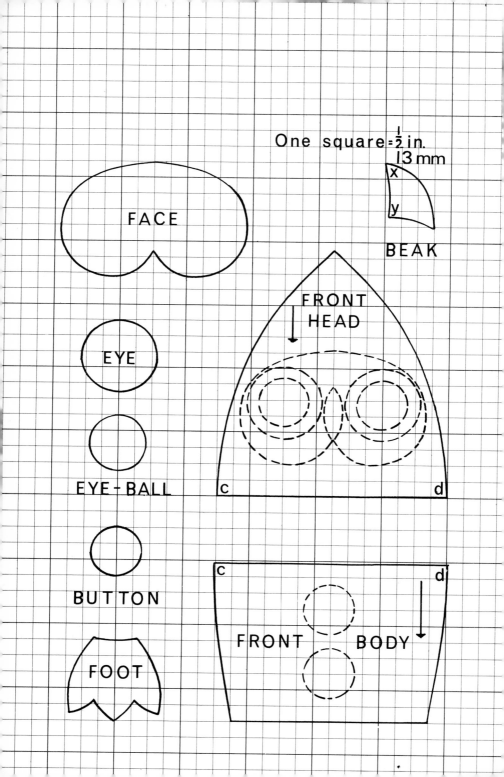

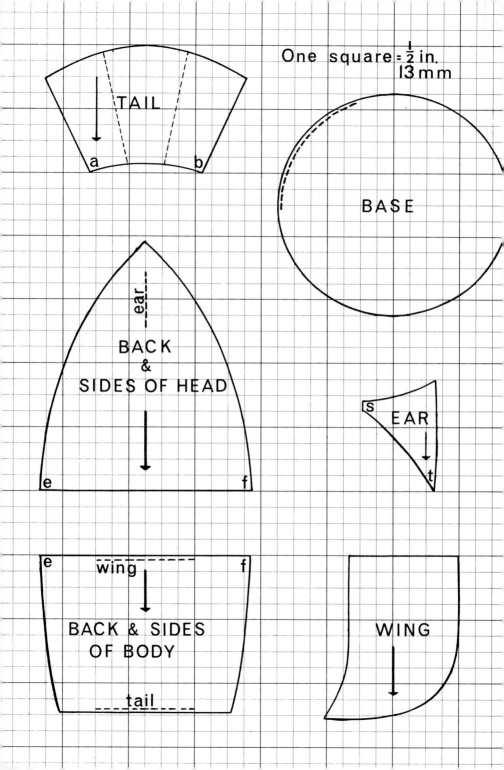

Owl

Materials

300 mm ($\frac{1}{3}$ yd) of printed cotton material for the body, wings and tail
230 mm ($\frac{1}{4}$ yd) of self-coloured cotton, velvet or light weight woollen material for the head and ears. Choose a colour which will complement the material selected for the body
A 150 mm (6 in.) square of white felt for the face
A 150 mm (6 in.) square of yellow, orange or red felt for the feet
A small piece of a bright coloured felt for the eyes and buttons
A small piece of black felt for the eyeballs
A small piece of felt for the beak
Either transparent or white glue
Stuffing approximately 280 grammes (10 oz).

To cut out

Make the paper patterns, using the diagram in which one square equals 13 mm ($\frac{1}{2}$ in.) as a guide. This size produces a toy 280 mm (11 in.) high. Cut the pattern pieces as follows:
Front Body   cut one in printed material
Back and sides of Body   cut three in printed material
Base   cut one in printed material
Tail   cut two in printed material
Wing   cut four in printed material
Front Head   cut one in self-coloured material
Back and sides of Head   cut three in self-coloured material
Face   cut one in white felt
Feet   cut four in yellow, orange or red felt
Beak   cut two in a bright coloured felt
Eye   cut two in a bright coloured felt
Button   cut two in a bright coloured felt
Eyeball   cut two in black felt
Ear   cut four in self-coloured material.

To make up

Sew each pair of wings together with right sides facing, leaving the straight edge open. Trim the points and turn to the right side. Stuff lightly to within 13 mm ($\frac{1}{2}$ in.) of the raw edges. Place each wing to the centre of two side body pieces in the position indicated by the dotted line on the pattern. The wings should face in opposite directions. Sew the wings to the side body pieces with right sides facing as close to the edge as possible.

Sew the two tail pieces together with right sides facing, leaving A to B open. Trim the points, turn to the right side and stuff very lightly to within 13 mm ($\frac{1}{2}$ in.) of the raw edges. Work two lines of stitching through all layers as indicated by the dotted lines on the tail pattern. Sew the tail to the back body piece with right sides facing, as close to the edge as possible in the position indicated by the dotted line on the pattern.

Sew the front head to the front body with right sides facing from C to D. Sew the back head to the back body with right sides facing from E to F. Sew the two side head pieces to the sides of the body with right sides facing from E to F, making sure that the seam is below the stitching used to sew the wing to the body. These four completed sections must now be sewn to each other along the curved edge and with right sides facing.

Sew each pair of feet together 3 mm ($\frac{1}{8}$ in.) from the edge, leaving the straight edge open. Trim the edges if necessary. Stuff the feet lightly. Sew to the bottom of the body 3 mm ($\frac{1}{8}$ in.) from the edge, with the centre of each foot placed to each of the front body seams.

Sew the base to the bottom of the body with right sides facing, leaving an opening of approximately 100 (4 in.) between the tail and one foot. Turn to the right side and stuff firmly. Sew up the opening with ladder stitch.

Sew each pair of ears together with right sides facing, leaving S to T open. Trim points and turn to the right side. Turn in the raw edges and oversew from S to T. Sew securely to the two side head pieces about 25 mm (1 in.) from the point where the four seams join, as indicated by the dotted line on the side head pattern.

Oversew the felt piece for the face to the front of the head in the position marked on the pattern. Sew the two beak pieces together 3 mm ($\frac{1}{8}$ in.) from the edge, leaving X to Y open. Stuff lightly and then sew to the face in the position marked on the pattern. Glue the eyeballs to the eyes and then glue to the face. Sew or glue the two felt buttons to the front body as shown by the dotted circles on the front body pattern.

ANIMAL POUFFES

larger toys for children to sit on, stand on, and climb over

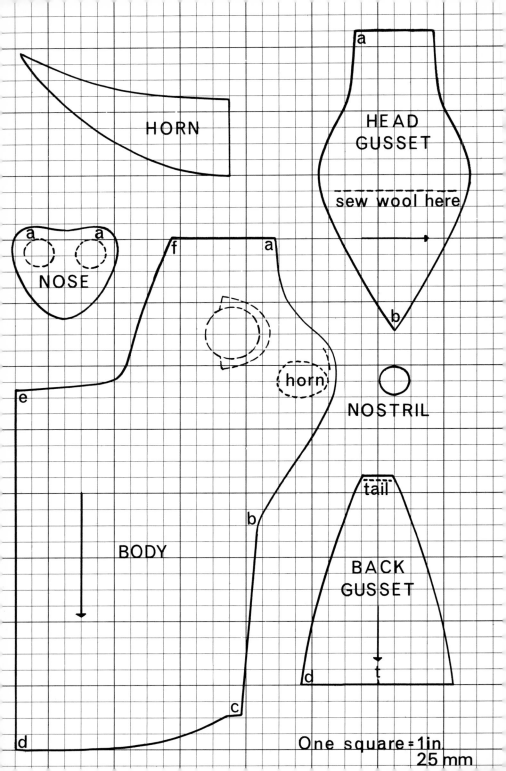

HORN

HEAD
GUSSET

sew wool here

a

NOSE

f   a

horn

b

NOSTRIL

e

tail

BODY

BACK
GUSSET

b

d   t

c

d

One square = 1 in
25 mm

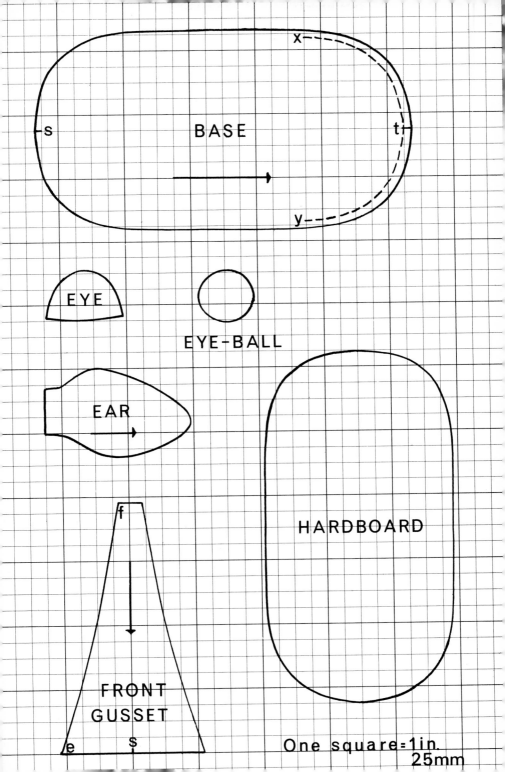

BASE

x

s   t

y

EYE

EYE-BALL

EAR

HARDBOARD

f

FRONT
GUSSET

e   s

One square=1in.
25mm

Highland cow

Materials

114 cm (1½ yd) of strong furnishing fabric 120 cm (48 in.) wide for the body. Choose a closely woven fabric that does not fray easily
230 mm (¼ yd) of white felt 815 mm (36 in.) wide for the horns and the eyes
230 mm (¼ yd) of a light coloured felt or plain cotton or woollen material for the nose and ear lining
A small piece of interlining for the ears
A 150 mm (6 in.) square of black felt for the nostrils and eye-balls
A 60 gramme (2 oz) hank of thick wool for the forelock and tail
Either transparent or white glue
A piece of hardboard cut to the template
Approximately 3 kg (7 lb) of wood wool.

To cut out

Make the paper patterns, using the diagram in which one square equals 25 mm (1 in.) as a guide. This size produces a pouffe 815 mm (32 in.) long and 510 mm (20 in.) high.
Cut the pattern pieces as follows:
Body   cut two in furnishing fabric
Base   cut one in furnishing fabric
Head Gusset   cut one in furnishing fabric
Back Gusset   cut one in furnishing fabric
Front Gusset   cut one in furnishing fabric
Ear   cut two in furnishing fabric
Ear   cut two in a plain material for the lining
Ear   cut two in interlining for stiffening
Nose   cut one in a plain material
Horn   cut four in white felt
Eye   cut two in white felt
Eyeball   cut two in black felt
Nostril   cut two in black felt.

To make up

It is extremely important that all the seams are very strong. It is therefore recommended that button thread is used for hand sewn seams or that two rows of machine stitching are worked on all the body seams. Half an inch is the seam allowance on the pouffes.

Cut through the hank of thick wool and lay it out straight. Cut a 300 mm (12 in.) length from one end for the forelock. The remainder of the wool is used for the tail. Sew the wool for the forelock to the head gusset in the position indicated by the dotted line on the pattern. The wool should be spread evenly across the head gusset and must be stitched very securely to it, with the stitching line half way along the wool. When the pouffe is finished the back half of the wool is folded forward to make a double thickness falling forwards. For the tail sew one end of the remainder of the wool to the back gusset in the position indicated on the pattern. As it may be frequently used to pull the pouffe along, make sure that it is very securely attached to the back gusset, preferably using machine stitching and working several rows backwards and forwards. Plait the wool to within 100 mm (4 in.) of the end; tie a length of wool very tightly at the end of the plaiting.

Place each ear piece and each ear lining together with right sides facing. Then place one piece of interlining on top of these two pieces. Sew all three layers together. Turn to the right side and press lightly. Repeat for the other ear. Fold each ear in half and sew securely to the body pieces just in front of the horns, as indicated by the dotted line on the pattern and 6 mm ($\frac{1}{4}$ in.) from the edge.

With right sides facing, sew each side of the head gusset to each body piece, matching A to A and B to B. Make sure that the wool for the forelock does not get caught in the seams. Sew along the back of the animal from B to C. With right sides facing, sew the back gusset to each side of the body, matching D to D. Point C on the body piece should match the centre of the top of the gusset. Make sure that the wool for the tail does not get caught in the seams. With right sides facing, sew the front gusset to each side of the body, matching E to E and F to F. Insert the nose piece with right sides facing. Sew together, matching A to A. It is important to position the nose piece centrally or the head will become lopsided. Sew the base to the bottom of the body with right sides facing, matching S to S and T to T. Leave an opening at the back of the body from X to Y to allow for the insertion of the piece of hardboard.

Turn the completed body to the right side and start to stuff the head. Use kapok or cotton flock to line the head first and then pack in the wood wool as hard as possible. Continue stuffing the rest of the body until about three quarters full. Insert the hardboard. Complete the stuffing. Sew up the opening with ladder stitch, using button thread.

Sew each pair of horns together, leaving the straight edge open. The stitching should be 3 mm ($\frac{1}{8}$ in.) from the edge. Stuff the horns with kapok or cotton flock very firmly. Sew the horns to each side of the head in the position marked on the pattern. Make sure that the horns are very securely attached to the head. Use button thread for strength and sew round each horn twice.

Glue the nostrils to the nose piece in the positions marked on the pattern. Glue the eyeballs to the eyes. Glue the eyes to the head in the positions marked on the pattern. Arrange the wool for the forelock so that both layers fall forwards. Trim if necessary.

Hen

Materials

910 mm (1 yd) of strong furnishing fabric 120 cm (48 in.) wide for the main part of the body. Choose a closely woven and preferably printed material.
460 mm ($\frac{1}{2}$ yd) of strong material 910 mm (36 in.) wide for the head. Choose a material which does not fray easily and a colour that either complements or contrasts with the material chosen for the body.
A 230 mm (9 in.) square of red or orange felt for the comb
A small piece of orange or yellow felt for the beak
A small piece of white felt for the eyes
A small piece of black felt for the eyeballs
Either transparent or white glue
A piece of hardboard cut to the template
Approximately 3 kg (7 lb) of wood wool for stuffing
A small quantity of kapok or cotton flock.

To cut out

Make the paper patterns, using the diagram in which one square equals 25 mm (1 in.) as a guide. This size produces a pouffe 660 mm (26 in.) long and 610 mm (24 in.) high. Cut the pattern pieces as follows:
Body   cut two in furnishing fabric
Base   cut one in furnishing fabric
Back Gusset   cut one in furnishing fabric
Front Gusset   cut one in furnishing fabric
Head   cut two in self-coloured material
Head Gusset   cut one in self-coloured material
Comb   cut two in red or orange felt
Beak   cut two in orange or yellow felt
Eye   cut two in white felt
Eyeball   cut two in black felt.

68

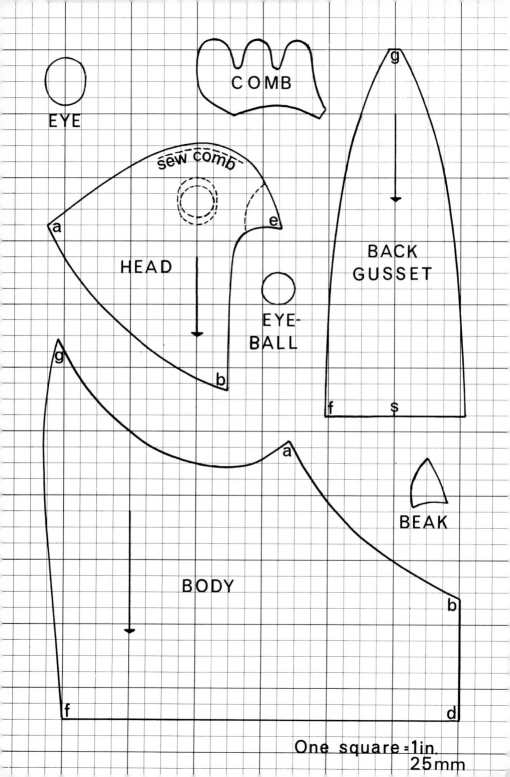

EYE

COMB

sew comb

HEAD

e

a

b

g

BACK
GUSSET

f   s

EYE-
BALL

g

a

BEAK

b

BODY

f   d

One square = 1in.
25mm

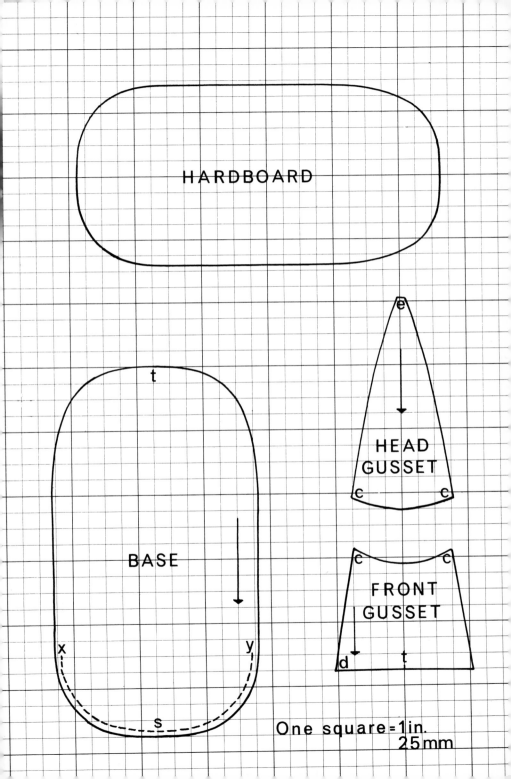

HARDBOARD

HEAD
GUSSET

t

BASE

x   y

s

e

c   c

c   c

FRONT
GUSSET

d   t

One square=1in.
25mm

To make up

It is extremely important that all the seams are very strong. It is therefore recommended that button thread is used for hand sewing or that two rows of machine stitching are worked on all the body seams. 13 mm ($\frac{1}{2}$ in.) is the seam allowance for the pouffes.

Glue the two felt pieces for the comb together and leave to dry. Sew each head piece to each body piece with right sides facing, matching A to A and B to B. Sew the head gusset to the front gusset with right sides facing, matching C to C. Sew this completed front piece to the head and body with right sides facing, matching D to D and E to E. Make sure that the join between the head and body materials and the join between the head and front gussets meets at the same point.

Sew the back gusset to each side of the body with right sides facing, matching F to F and G to G. Tack the felt comb to one side of the head in the position indicated by the dotted line on the pattern. Sew the head and body together from G to E. Sew the base to the body with right sides facing, matching S to S and T to T. Leave an opening at the back of the body from X to Y to allow for the insertion of the hardboard. Turn the completed body to the right side and start to stuff the head and tail. Use a little kapok or cotton flock to stuff the point for the beak and the narrow part of the tail. Then continue stuffing the rest of the body with wood wool, packing it in as hard as possible. Insert the piece of hardboard when the pouffe is about three quarters filled with wood wool. Complete the stuffing and sew up the opening with ladder stitch and button thread.

Oversew the two felt pieces for the beak together, put a little kapok or cotton flock into the point; place over the head and stitch securely to the material.

Glue the eyeballs to the eyes. Then glue to the head in the position indicated on the pattern.

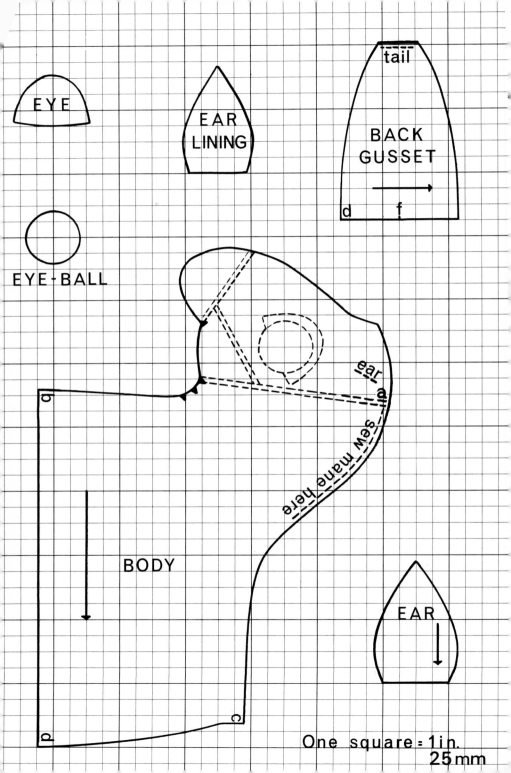

EYE

EYE-BALL

EAR
LINING

BACK
GUSSET

tail

d   f

ear

sew mane here

a

BODY

q

p   c

EAR

One square = 1 in.
25 mm

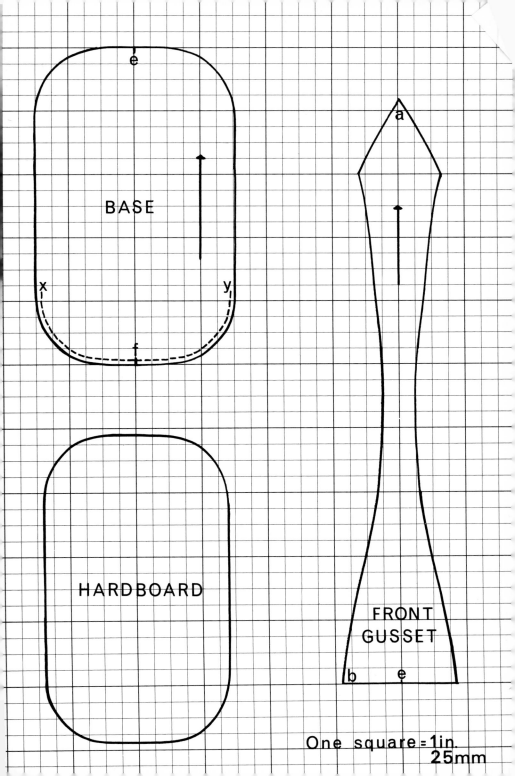

BASE

x   y

e

f

HARDBOARD

a

FRONT
GUSSET

b   e

One square = 1in.
25mm

Horse

Materials

114 mm (1½ yds) of strong furnishing fabric 120 cm (48 in.) wide for the body
Choose a closely woven fabric that does not fray easily.
A small piece of interlining for the ears
A 230 mm (9 in.) square of white felt for the eyes
A 220 mm (9 in.) square of black felt for the eyeballs
Two 60 gramme (2 oz) hanks of thick wool for the mane and tail
274 cm (3 yds) of ribbon or braid 25 mm (1 in.) wide for the reins
Either transparent or white glue
A piece of hardboard cut to the template
Approximately 3 kg (7 lb) wood wool for stuffing
Small quantity of kapok or cotton flock.

To cut out

Make the paper patterns, using the diagram in which one square equals 25 mm (1 in.) as a guide. This size produces a pouffe 790 mm (31 in.) long and 530 mm (21 in.) high.
Cut the pattern pieces as follows:
Body   cut two in furnishing fabric
Base   cut one in furnishing fabric
Front Gusset   cut one in furnishing fabric
Back Gusset   cut one in furnishing fabric
Ear   cut four in furnishing fabric
Ear   cut two in interlining
Eye   cut two in white felt
Eyeball   cut two in black felt.

76

To make up

It is extremely important that all the seams are very strong. It is therefore recommended that button thread is used for hand sewing or that two rows of machine stitching are worked on all the body seams. 13 mm ($\frac{1}{2}$ in.) is the seam allowance for the pouffes.

Cut through one of the hanks of thick wool and lay it out straight. Cut a 460 mm (18 in.) length from one end for the forelock. The remainder of the hank is used for the tail and the other hank is required for the mane. Fold the length of wool for the tail in half and sew the folded end to the top of the back gusset. The wool must be very securely attached to the material as the pouffe will be frequently pulled along by its tail. It is preferable to use machine stitching and work several rows backwards and forwards over the wool. Plait the wool to within 100 mm (4 in.) of the end. Tie a ribbon or strand of wool very tightly at the end of the plaiting.

Fold the 460 mm (18 in.) length of wool for the forelock in half and sew securely to one of the body pieces at point A. Using the whole of the other hank of wool, make the mane as follows: With the right side of one body piece facing you, loop the wool closely together, making the loops about 100 mm (4 in.) long and pinning each loop as it is made. Make a series of loops, extending from point A and immediately behind the forelock, along the back of the neck as indicated by the dotted line marked on the pattern. Tack the loops in place about 6 mm ($\frac{1}{4}$ in.) from the edge of the material. Then sew very securely. It is preferable to machine stitch the loops of wool to the material as they will have to withstand a good deal of tugging. Having secured mane, tail and forelock, the body pieces can now be sewn together.

With right sides facing sew the front gusset to each side of the body, matching A to A and B to B. Make sure that the wool does not get caught in the seams. It is best to sew each side, starting from the same point to avoid any possible puckering. Snip the seam at the points marked on the pattern, taking care not to cut the stitching. Sew along the back of the body from A to C. Make sure that the loops for the mane are neatly arranged, as they can get disturbed by the stitching, particularly if machine stitching is used.

With right sides facing, sew the back gusset to each side of the body, matching D to D. Point C on the body piece should match the centre of the top of the gusset. Make sure that the wool for the tail does not get caught in the seams.

Sew the base to the bottom of the body with right sides facing, matching E to E and F to F. Leave an opening at the back of the body from X to Y to allow for the insertion of the hardboard. Turn the completed body to the right side and start to stuff the head. Use kapok or cotton flock to line the head first and then pack in the wood wool as hard as possible. Continue stuffing the rest of the body until about three quarters full. Then insert the piece of hardboard. Complete the stuffing and sew up the opening with ladder stitch, using button thread.

Place two ear pieces together with right sides facing. Place one piece of interlining on the top. Then sew all three layers together, leaving the straight edge open. Trim the point and then turn to the right side. Turn in the raw edges and oversew together. Fold each ear in half and sew very securely to each side of the head in the position marked on the pattern.

Glue or sew lengths of ribbon or braid to the head to make the harness. Measure the required lengths with a tape measure and then cut four pieces from the ribbon or braid. One piece goes round the nose. One piece goes right round the head, under the chin and behind the ears. The other two pieces are smaller lengths which join the former two pieces together. The remainder of the ribbon or braid is for the reins. The reins are attached to either side of the nose. Refer to the diagram and to the illustration for the positioning of the harness and the reins.

Glue the eyeballs to the eyes. Then glue the eyes to the head in the position indicated on the pattern. Trim the forelock and the end of the tail. The loops for the mane can either be left as they are or cut through if desired.

BIBLIOGRAPHY

Introducing Soft Toy Making Delphine Davidson Batsford London Praeger New York

Modern Soft Toy Making Margaret Hutchings Mills and Boon London Branford Newton Center Massachusetts

Dolls and How to Make Them Margaret Hutchings Mills and Boon London Branford Newton Center Massachusetts

Simple Toymaking Sheila Jackson Studio Vista London Watson-Guptill New York

Make your Own Dolls Ilse Strobl-Wohlschlager Batsford London Van Nostrand Reinhold New York

Making Felt Toys and Glove Puppets Suzy Ives Batsford London Branford Newton Center Massachusetts

Printed Rag Toys Joy Wilcox Batsford London

Making Soft Toys Gillian Lockwood Studio Vista London Watson-Guptill New York

SUPPLIERS

Felt, fur fabric, kapok, glass eyes, etc

Fred Aldous Limited   The Handicraft Centre   PO Box 135
    37 Lever Street   Manchester   M60 1UX
Arts and Crafts   10 Byram Street   Huddersfield   HD1 1DA
Dryad Handicrafts Limited   Northgates   Leicester
Home Pastimes Handicrafts   69 Mansfield Road   Nottingham
Leighton, Baldwin and Cox   41 High Street
    Leighton Buzzard   Bedfordshire
Nottingham Handicraft Company   Melton Road
    West Bridgford   Nottingham
The Needlewoman Shop   146 Regent Street   London   W1

Felt, large quantities only

B Brown Limited   Warreniner House   Greville Street
    London EC1
Bury and Masco Industries Limited   PO Box 14
    Hudcar Mills   Bury   Lancashire

Remnants

J W Coates and Company Limited   Department E B1
    Nelson   Lancashire
Pater Textiles   Department WR9   19 Rampart Street
    London E1

Wool

John Deacon Limited   9–11 Peckover Street   Bradford 1
Herbert Smith (Hermit) Limited   89–93 Caledonia Street
    Bradford 5

Kapok and other fillings

Branches of Woolworth's

Kapok and other fillings in bulk only

Abbey Kapok Manufacturing Company Limited   Selinas Lane
    Dagenham   Kent
Arkinson's   Church Street   Preston   Lancashire

Glues

White cement   Copydex   Marvin Medium   UHU
    Clear Bostik
available from most handicraft and hardware stores.